Tunisian Cr

Pauline Turner

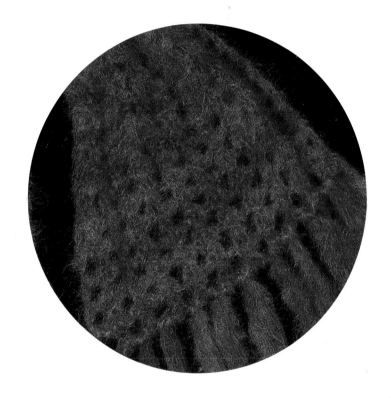

Search Press

Introduction

Tunisian crochet is a unique combination of knitting and crochet techniques and produces fabrics which have the characteristics and appearance of both crafts. The finished effect is a textile that looks rather like a woven fabric on the right side, whilst the back has an appearance very similar to the reverse side of knitted stocking stitch.

Until recently, Tunisian crochet has largely been ignored in the UK, although it is well-known in the USA. This is because many of the patterns published in Britain have used the same-sized Tunisian hook to work a design, as would be used to produce a similar item in knitting or crochet. This has resulted in very stiff fabrics which are heavy, and therefore expensive, as they use more yarn than normal. This clumsy fabric is also rather difficult to work, because of the tightness of the tension. In fact, all the fun has been taken out of what should be an interesting and practical aspect of crochet techniques.

The remedy is simple! By using a larger-sized Tunisian hook than would normally be recommended when knitting or crocheting in a particular yarn, I have found that a softer, easier to work, and therefore more economical design can be produced. It is the intention of this book to encourage all those who have previously been dissatisfied with the results obtained by this technique, and those who have never even attempted it, to explore its tremendous possibilities.

Tools and materials

Just as with other crochet techniques, the tools and materials you will need to begin experimenting are minimal. The basic requirements are a Tunisian hook, suitable yarn, a measuring tape, pins, scissors and blunt-ended needles for sewing up seams.

TUNISIAN HOOKS

Tunisian crochet is worked on a special hook that is as long as a knitting needle. These are called Tunisian crochet hooks, or tricot hooks and, in America, they are often referred to as Afghan hooks. These hooks can be purchased in different metric sizes and lengths. The smaller the metric figure shown, the finer the hook and the tighter the tension obtained.

Because of the very dense nature of Tunisian crochet fabric, it is essential to use a hook two or more sizes larger than would normally be recommended for knitting or crocheting with a specific yarn. As an example, where a 4.00 metric hook or needles are given for use with a double knitting quality, try working with a 5.00, 5.50, or even a 6.00 hook to produce a lighter fabric.

For extremely wide areas of crochet, such as Afghan rugs, blankets and bedspreads, Flexi-hooks are needed. These have a short, hooked end, similar to an ordinary crochet hook, with a long wire and stopper attached.

Double-ended Tunisian hooks are also manufactured and these produce fabrics of a different texture to ordinary hooks. One advantage is that they can be used to work a reversible fabric in two colours. On one side, the first colour will predominate but on the other side, the second colour will be more distinct. When using normal Tunisian hooks, the fabric has a tendency to curl until a border has been added, because the work is not turned and the right side remains facing throughout. When a double-ended hook is used, however, the work *is* turned and so cancels out the curl. Another use is when working a border all round a garment without a break. By working the border with a double-ended hook, it is possible to pick up the stitches with one ball of yarn and, once sufficient loops are on the hook, take them off again at the other end with a second ball of yarn, (see Fig 1).

MATERIALS

All of the yarns available for normal knitting and crochet methods are suitable for Tunisian crochet designs. These qualities include pure wool, synthetics, blends of wool and synthetics, soft cottons, mohair, glitter yarns and such fibres as raffia and string for unusual textures.

The main point to stress in the choice of yarn is that lightweight qualities are more suitable for most fashion garments and accessories. Soft cottons and acrylics are also ideal for household items. Remember, the thicker and harsher the fibres, the tighter and stiffer the texture of the fabric.

first ball of yarn

fig 1

second ball of yarn ready to turn

Basic steps

Tunisian crochet is also often referred to as Tunisian knitting. This is very understandable as to produce the fabric you have to pick up the loops in one direction, as though you were knitting, then take them off in the other direction, as if you were crocheting. This technique, however, does not contradict the principle that all crochet begins and ends with a single loop on the hook, no matter how complicated the process in between.

As with all knitting and crochet, this method begins with a slip knot. A chain is then made to give the exact number of stitches needed for the section of work, excluding the loop on the hook. Unlike ordinary crochet, there is no need for a turning chain at the beginning of a row when picking up the loops. One half row is now worked to pick up the loops, whilst another half row removes those loops – so completing one row and bringing the work back to one loop on the hook. A word of warning at this

point may not go amiss, as some designers describe the picking up and taking off of the loops as two separate rows. Others, myself included, think of the picking up and taking off as one process and, therefore, just one row. In this book, the instructions give the pick-up row as half a row, abbreviated as 'pur', and the take-off row as half a row, abbreviated as 'tor'. *Note:* the list of abbreviations can be found on page 32.

BASIC TUNISIAN STITCH

Although texture can quite easily be introduced into a Tunisian crochet fabric, the basic, and most common stitch, is the one known as 'Tunisian simple stitch', and it gives this type of crochet its characteristic look, (see page 8).

To practice this stitch, use a Tunisian hook up to four times larger than the one recommended on the ball band for a pair of knitting needles. Make the exact number of chains you require.

Pick-up foundation row: Insert the hook into the second chain, picking up the top strand only of the chain and not two loops as would be the case with ordinary crochet, yarn over hook and draw through the chain loop. Leave this loop on the hook, noting that there should now be two loops on the hook. *Insert the hook into the next chain, yarn over hook, draw through to front of work, leave this loop on the hook, repeat from * until all the chain has been used, (see Fig 2). Check the number of stitches at this point and make sure they are the same as the commencing chain.

fig 2

Take-off foundation row: Yarn over hook, pull through one loop only, noting that this is the equivalent of a turning chain and makes it easier to keep the left-hand edge straight, *yarn over hook and pull through two loops, repeat from * to end of row. The yarn collected in the hook head pulls through the working loop just made and one of the loops on the hook, (see Fig 3), indicated by (a).

One row of Tunisian simple stitch has now been completed. This provides the base to begin making the fabric, as there is now a vertical strand of yarn at the front of each stitch, just below the hook.

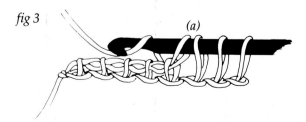

fig 3   *(a)*

Next and subsequent rows: To pick up the stitches again, do not make a turning chain but think of this half of the row as following knitting principles. The loop on the hook is the stitch for the first vertical strand, so insert the hook under the next vertical strand, (see Fig 4), yarn over hook, pull through to give second loop on hook, *insert hook under next vertical strand, yarn over hook, pull through and leave on hook, repeat from * to end of row, noting that it is quite easy to miss the last strand, so make sure that strand (a) has been worked into, (see Fig 4).

To take off loops, work 1ch, *yarn over hook, pull through two loops, repeat from * to end of row, until one loop only remains.

(a)   *fig 4*

TO INCREASE A STITCH

At the position for the increase, before picking up the next vertical strand, insert the hook under the horizontal strands lying between the stitch on the hook and the next stitch, collect yarn in hook head and pull through on to the hook in the usual way – one increase has been made – then continue in Tunisian simple stitch, (see Fig 5).

fig 5

TO DECREASE A STITCH

There are different methods of decreasing but I have found the following to be the least confusing. At the position for the decrease, decrease on the pick-up action by inserting the hook under two vertical strands at the same time, yarn over hook and pull through both strands at once. This leaves only one loop over two stitches on the hook and one stitch has been decreased.

FINISHING OFF IN BASIC TUNISIAN SIMPLE STITCH

Use an ordinary crochet hook two sizes smaller than the size of Tunisian hook being used. A large hook will create a frilly edge, similarly, inserting the hook through the whole fabric, which is normal in double crochet, leaves holes. Continue to pick up only the vertical strands, that is, one loop and not two as in ordinary crochet, and double crochet to the end. The only instance when this method would not be used is if two seams need to be joined invisibly.

RIGHT SIDE OF FABRIC

Unlike ordinary flat crochet, Tunisian crochet is worked with the right side of the fabric always facing you, unless using a method that requires a double-ended Tunisian hook. This means that the fabric will curl while it is being worked, but most designs have edges added at the making up stage which will counteract this curl.

JOINING IN YARN

Whether changing to a new colour, or joining in a new ball of the main shade, leave sufficient length on both balls. These two ends can then be oversewn into the back of the loops of the stitches. As a general rule, the yarn end at the right of the hook will be oversewn to the left of the work, and the yarn at the left of the hook will be oversewn into the stitches at the right of the work.

WATCH POINTS

Variations to the basic Tunisian stitch and methods are numerous but before going on to some of the more exciting aspects of this technique, it is worth looking at three points which are the cause of some concern.

Bias effect: As the fabric is produced, it may lean either to the right, or to the left, so that it is not a true square. Normally, the slant will be to the right.
Solution: Check that the hook is being inserted into the second vertical strand at the beginning of a pick-up row and not into the strand immediately below the loop already on the hook. Alternatively, check that you have picked up the very last vertical strand of the row.

Loss of stitches: This is a common fault, particularly when increasing or decreasing.
Solution: Make sure that on a pick-up row you are picking up the last vertical strand and that at the beginning of the row, you are working into the second vertical strand and not the third. On the taking-off row, check that when the yarn is put over the hook it is pulled through two loops and not three.

Tension: You may find that the width tension is easy to obtain but that the given number of rows will not produce the correct length.
Solution: As with normal crochet, the hook should sit at the top of the work, so on a pick-up row, check that the hook is being lifted up to the top of the row, rather than letting it lie in front of the work. If the hook is not lifted clear of the fabric, the tension is tighter and the rows shorter. Another way of counteracting too tight a tension is to make sure that the yarn hand is pulling away from the hook during the taking-off of the loops. One further point is to check how you are holding the Tunisian hook. I find it better to hold the hook well away from the actual hook head, with my hand on top of the hook as in knitting. With this method, I create a looser and more exciting tension.

Projects in Tunisian simple stitch

Having mastered the basics of this technique, it is now time to decide what you want to make. I am quite sure that instead of just making little samples until a level of perfection has been reached, you would much rather make a reasonably simple item and have something to show for your efforts.

The following suggestions are easy to execute and simple to assemble but I am sure that with a little practice, you will want to experiment with your own ideas.

CUSHION COVERS

Make a cushion cover in Tunisian simple stitch, working the back in one colour and the front in stripes. Use as many different colours as you can find, working one row in each colour. This is a marvellous way of using up oddments of yarn.

Another suggestion is to work the back in Tunisian simple stitch in one colour, then progress to some of the more unusual stitches given in the following pages, and work the front in one of these using a contrasting or toning yarn.

When you have completed both pieces, put them together with the wrong sides facing each other. Work in double crochet through both of the pieces round three of the four sides, so that they are joined together. Continue in double crochet along the fourth side of one of the pieces only, to allow for an opening. Before breaking off the yarn, trim with a row of crab stitch, working in double crochet from left to right instead of from right to left as with normal double crochet, round all four sides. Fasten off. Insert cushion pad and close the opening with the same yarn and a blunt-ended sewing needle, or insert a zip fastener.

TUBULAR SCARVES

Work in Tunisian simple stitch, or any of the stitches described in the following pages, and make a length of crochet 50in (127cm) or more and double the required width of the finished scarf. Fasten off.

With the wrong sides facing you, sew, or double crochet the two long edges together to form a tube, turn to the right side. Neatly join the two short edges and either add a fringe to each end, or gather the ends up and trim with huge tassles or pompons.

PATCHWORK DESIGNS

To make colourful designs, work lots of small squares in Tunisian simple stitch, all to the same size but in different colours and yarn textures. If you want to be adventurous try working some of the squares in the stitches described in the following pages.

For a shopping bag: Use a dishcloth cotton, or some similar hardwearing fibre for this project.

For a cushion cover: Join all the patches together, then complete as given for the cushion cover.

For a pram cover: Join the patches together to give the correct size and work an edging all round in one colour.

For an Afghan rug: Make patches of different stitches and join them together as a reminder of your progress.

Jacket in Tunisian simple stitch

The fronts and back of this jacket are worked in one piece to the underarms, then divided and completed separately. The contrasting borders and shoulder insets are worked in ordinary crochet, (see page 8).

Materials: 300g of DK in main colour; 50g of DK in contrasting colour; one 8.00mm Tunisian hook; one 6.00mm crochet hook.

Size: To fit 36″ (92cm) bust. To increase or reduce the size, add or subtract 4 sts on the foundation row. When dividing at the underarms, allow 2 sts more or less for the back and one st for each front.

Tension: 12 sts = 4″ (10cm) on 8.00mm Tunisian hook.

BODY

With 8.00mm hook and M make 108 ch. Work 9 rows Ts on these 108 sts.

Row 10: Dec 2 tog over 26th/27th sts; 45th/46th sts; 63rd/64th sts and 81st/82nd sts, (104 sts). Work 3 rows Ts.

Row 14: Dec 2 tog over 25th/26th sts; 43rd/44th sts; 60th/61st sts and 77th/78th sts, (100 sts). Work 18 rows Ts or until piece measures 13½″ (34cm) from beginning.

RIGHT FRONT

Work 2 rows Ts on the first 19 sts for the right front.

Next row: Dec 2 tog, Ts to end, (18 sts). Repeat the last 3 rows 5 times more. Work 7 rows on remaining 13 sts. Fasten off.

BACK

Miss first 8 sts and rejoin yarn to next st. Work 22 rows Ts over 46 sts. Fasten off.

LEFT FRONT

Miss first 8 sts and rejoin yarn to next st. Work 2 rows Ts on the remaining 19 sts.

Next row: Ts to last 3 sts, dec 2 tog, 1Ts in last st. Repeat the last 3 rows 5 times more. Work 7 rows Ts on remaining 13 sts. Fasten off.

SHOULDER INSETS

With 6.00mm crochet hook and M work 27dc down front armhole edge. Connect last st to first missed st of Tunisian st, ss over 2 missed Tunisian sts, 1tr in dc, work in tr to end, join in contrast.

**Next row: With Rs facing, 1ch, 1dc, *miss 4 sts, beg at the bottom of the stem of the next tr and putting the sts just above each other, work 1 quad tr, 1tr tr, 1dtr, 1tr all round same stem with 1dc at top of same st, rep from * to end, ss into next Tunisian missed st. Fasten off.

***Next row: With Rs facing, pick up M still connected and place *1dc in dc, 1tr in each of the unused main tr lying behind the contrast colour, rep from * to end, connect M to missed Tunisian st, (3 Tunisian sts unworked). Work 1 row dc. Fasten off. Work other side to match. Join shoulder seams.

SLEEVES (MAKE 2)

With 8.00mm hook and M make 56 ch and beg at top. Work 18 rows Ts. Work 2 rows Ts.

Next row: Work in Ts, dec one st at each end of row. Repeat the last 3 rows 3 times more. 48 sts. Work 3 rows Ts. Commence cuff. Change to 6.00mm crochet hook and work 1 row dc.

Next row: 3ch, 1tr into each st to end.

Next row: In contrast colour, as ** of inset.

Next row: In M, as *** of inset.

Next row: In crab st to end. Fasten off. Join sleeve seams. Set in sleeves to armholes.

BORDERS

With Rs of work facing, 6.00mm crochet hook and M, beg at centre back neck and work in dc round neck, dec 2 tog at neck corner and shoulder, dc down front working 3dc in corner, dc along base edge picking up vertical strands, work 3dc in corner, dc up front dec 2 tog over shoulder and back neck corner, dc to end, join with ss.
To ensure that the border is balanced, count front border sts and mark with pins before working with the contrast yarn. Work the last 4 rows of the cuff instructions to complete the border.

Simple-to-make jacket
Basic Tunisian crochet is
used to make this
attractive jacket. A slightly
more elaborate border in
ordinary crochet is added
for effect

Mohair scarf
Tunisian lace stitch worked in
mohair on a large hook

Lace techniques

Openwork stitches which have the appearance of true crochet are simple to work by the Tunisian method. Unlike simple stitch, however, they require exact multiples of stitches to make them work out correctly.

Using a fine, soft yarn, these stitches make beautiful baby garments. I have chosen a random-dyed mohair and Tunisian cluster lace to make the stole shown on page 9. You will need a 10mm Tunisian hook, about 200g of mohair and begin with 48 ch. When you have sufficient length, finish off the sides edges with double crochet and add luxurious fringes to both ends.

TUNISIAN CLUSTER LACE

Make a number of chains divisible by 4.
Pick up the foundation loops as for simple stitch.
On the next take-off row, yoh and pull through first 2 loops on hook, *4ch, yoh and pull through 5 loops, rep from * to last 3 sts on hook, 3ch, yoh and pull through 3 loops on hook. On the next pick-up row work 1ch, pick up loops by inserting hook into each chain only, yoh, pull yarn through and leave loop on hook.
Repeat from ** to ** to form pattern, ending with a take-off row, (see Fig 6).

TUNISIAN FILET LACE

Make a number of chains divisible by 2 plus one, eg 23.

Pick-up foundation row: Yarn round hook twice, insert hook into the 3rd ch from hook, yoh and draw through a loop, yoh and draw through first 2 loops on hook, *yarn round hook twice, miss next ch, insert hook into next ch, yoh and draw through a loop, yoh and draw through first 2 loops on hook, rep from * to end.

Take-off foundation row: 1ch, yoh and draw through first loop only, *yoh, pull through next 2 loops, rep from * to end.

Pick-up pattern row: 2ch, *yarn round hook twice, insert hook into both the next vertical loop and the slightly sloping vertical loop to the *right* of it which was made in the previous row, yoh and draw a loop through, yoh and draw through first 2 loops on hook, rep from * to end.

Take-off pattern row: As take-off foundation row.
The pattern pick-up and take-off rows are repeated to form the pattern, ending with a take-off row.

fig 6

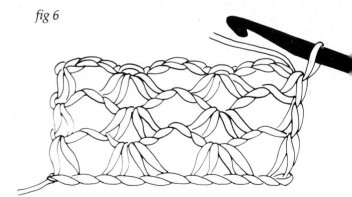

Coloured Techniques

Colourful fabrics are easy to produce and even Tunisian simple stitch takes on a completely different appearance when single stripes of colour are introduced at the point when all the loops have been removed from the hook. When changing colour at this point, do so whilst removing the very last loop from the previous row. If you change the colour when all the loops have been taken off there will be a colour 'drag' (see Fig 7a).

You can create a tweed pattern by picking up the loops with one colour and taking them off with another. For a multi-coloured tweed effect, bring in four, or more, toning or contrasting colours and alternate them throughout the fabric.

When narrow bands, or small areas of a single colour are blended with the tweed pattern, a variety of effects can be achieved. This is a marvellous way of using up many oddments of different colours.

Complex colour blending is produced by using small lengths of yarn to work part of a row only, as with jacquard crochet. With this method, the threads have to be woven in at the back of the work, or separate balls of yarn used for each block of colour and twisted round each other before proceeding with the next colour.

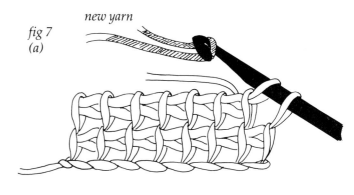

fig 7 (a)   new yarn

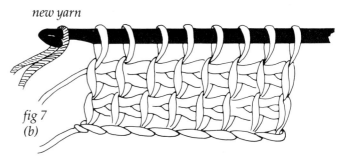

new yarn   fig 7 (b)

smaller hook, complete the piece by working in double crochet to the end.

TUNISIAN TWEED STITCH

Make any number of chains with the main colour. Pick up the foundation loops with this colour as for simple stitch.

Join in the next colour (see Fig 7b). Work one chain and take off the loops, then using the same colour pick up the loops again. Take off the loops with the first colour, then using the same colour pick up the loops again.

Repeat from ** to ** until the length of work has been completed, either working with two colours only, or bringing in more colours as required. Finish by taking off the loops with the main colour. Using a

Cross-over top

Tunisian tweed stitch is used for the main panels of this design. The two main sections are the same for all sizes; only the waistband stitches vary in number, (see page 16).

Materials: Aran thickness is used throughout, (or use any equivalent quality which will give the same tension); 300g of brown Aran yarn; 150g of cream Aran yarn; one 8.00mm Tunisian hook; one 6.50mm crochet hook.

Size: To fit bust sizes from 30-44" (76-110cm).

Tension: 5 sts = 2" (5cm) on 8.00mm Tunisian hook.

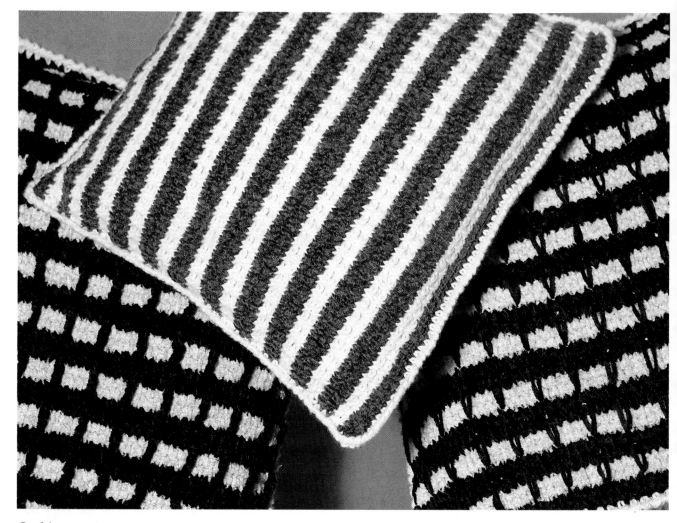

Cushions
The black and cream cushions illustrate two different ways to form boxes of
colour, either by dropping the stitch two rows below and inserting the hook
through the work, or by working a long Tunisian treble and picking up the
vertical strand in the top of the last main coloured stripe. The green and cream
cushion shows stripes worked in different yarn textures.

Teenager's jersey
Tunisian simple stitch and different colours
have been combined to create this attractive jersey

BODY SECTION (MAKE 2)

With 8.00mm hook and brown yarn, make 33ch. Pick up loops. Using cream as contrast, work in tweed simple stitch until work measures 28" (70cm).

Break off cream yarn. Using 6.50m crochet hook make 1 ch with brown yarn, work in dc along side edge of rectangle, placing 1 dc in each row end and picking up one of the horizontal strands as well as the usual vertical strands.

Next row: 1ch, turn, work in dc to end.
Work 2 more rows in dc. Work 1 row crab st. Fasten off.

With Rs facing, join brown yarn to other side of rectangle. Make second border to match, picking up the two strands that look like a ch.

TO MAKE UP

Place the two rectangles on a flat surface, (see Fig 8). Cross one over the other until the lapped edge measures half the required waist size, (eg, if waist is 30" (72cm), overlap the pieces to measure 15" (36cm) across the base of the rectangles).

fig 8

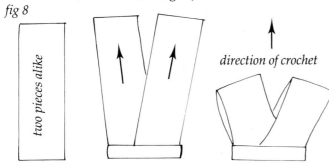

two pieces alike

direction of crochet

With Rs facing, 6.50mm crochet hook and brown yarn, join with a ss to the corner st and commence welt.

Work 1 row tr working into each st, with an even number of sts, turn, noting that part of the row will be worked into one thickness of Tunisian tweed st, the central section through two thicknesses and the remainder into one thickness. Work in raised tr rib for the required depth of welt as follows:

Next row: 3ch to count as first tr, miss first st, *insert hook from right to left round the stem of the next tr at the front of the work, work 1tr, *insert the hook from right to left round the stem of the next tr at the back of the work, work 1tr, rep from * to last tr, rep from * to *, turn.
Repeat this row as required. Fasten off.

Overlap the other edges of the rectangles in the same way but this time cross them in opposite directions, keeping the welt already worked nearest to you. This means that the right hand rectangle always overlaps the left hand rectangle, as long as you have followed the directions in Fig 8.

Teenager's Jersey

The choice of greys spiced with black and white make this striking design particularly suitable for a boy, (see page 13). It would, however, look just as effective in bright, bold contrasting colours.

Materials: 300g DK in medium grey (M); 50g light grey (A); 100g black (B); 25g white (C); one 7.00mm Tunisian hook; one 4.50mm crochet hook.

Size: To fit 34" (86cm) bust/chest.

Tension: 7 sts and 6 rows = 2" (5cm) worked on 7.00mm Tunisian hook.

BACK

With 7.00mm hook and M make 60 ch. Work 3 rows Ts.

Row 4: Pick up in M. Break off M. Take off in B. Work 3 rows Ts in B.

Row 8: Pick up in B. Break off B. Rejoin M. Take off in M.
Work 4 rows Ts in M.

Row 13: Pick up in M. Break off M. Join in A. Take off in A.

Row 14: Work 1 row Ts in A, do not break off yarn.

Row 15: Join in B. Work 1 row Ts in B. Break off B.

Row 16: Work 1 row Ts in A.

Row 17: Pick up in A. Break off A. Rejoin M. Take off in M.
Work 4 rows Ts in M.
Using M and B in the same row, commence pattern, noting that M is twisted behind the sts in B, as in Fair Isle knitting to avoid long strands of yarn.

Row 22: Pick up 7 in M, *6 in B, 4 in M, rep from * to last 3 sts, 3 in M. Take off in same manner as pick up.

Row 23: Pick up 6 in M, *6 in B, 4 in M, rep from * to last 4 sts, 4 in M. Take off keeping colours correct.

Row 24: Pick up 5 in M, *6 in B, 4 in M, rep from * to last 5 sts, 5 in M. Take off keeping colours correct.

Row 25: As row 23.

Row 26: As row 22. Break off B.
Work 4 rows Ts in M.

Rows 31-35: As rows 13-17.
Work 4 rows Ts in M.

Rows 40-44: As rows 4-8.
Work 4 rows Ts in M.

Row 49: Using M and B, pick up *6 in B, 4 in M, rep from * to end. Take off keeping colours correct.

Row 50: Pick up 1 in M, *6 in B, 4 in M, rep from * to end, working only 3 in M at end. Take off keeping colours correct.

Row 51: Pick up 2 in M, *6 in B, 4 in M, rep from * to end, working only 2 in M at end. Take off keeping colours correct.

Row 52: As row 50.

Row 53: As row 49. Break off B.
Work 4 rows Ts in M.

Row 58; Pick up in M. Take off in B.
Work 8 rows Ts in B. Fasten off.

FRONT

Work as given for back. Do not join side seams yet. Join 10 sts at each side of top edges for shoulders, leaving 40 sts free for neck.

NECK EDGING

With 4.50mm crochet hook, join B to shoulder seam. Work 4 rows raised treble rib, see welt of Cross-over top, page 16. Fasten off.
As an alternative edging, with 4.00mm knitting needles, pick up and work 6 rows single rib. Cast off.

SLEEVES (MAKE 2)

With 7.00mm hook and B pick up 54 sts between rows 40 on back and front, over the shoulder seam. Take off in B.
Work 8 rows Ts in B.

Row 10: Pick up in B. Take off in M.

Row 11: Dec one st at each end of row, picking up and taking off in M. 52 sts.
Work 4 rows Ts in M.

Row 16: Dec one st at each end of row, picking up in M and taking off in A.

Row 17: Work in A.

Row 18: Work in C.

Row 19: Work in A.

Row 20: Pick up in A. Take off in M.

Row 21: Dec one st at each end of row, picking up and taking off in M.
Work 4 rows Ts in M.

Row 26: Dec one st at each end of row, picking up in M and taking off in B.
Work 3 rows Ts in B.

Row 30: Pick up in B. Take off in M.

Row 31: Dec one st at each end of row, picking up and taking off in M.

Cross-over top
Panels of two colours of
yarn blended to give a
tweed effect

Mohair waistcoat
A large hook and small
amounts of mohair are
blended for a colourful
effect. Many different
Tunisian crochet stitches
are used and the design is
worked from the side

Work 4 rows Ts in M.

Rows 36-50: As rows 16-30. 36 sts.

Row 51: Dec one st at each end of row, picking up and taking off in M.
Work 10 rows Ts in M. (Adjust sleeve length here.)
Change to 4.50mm crochet hook and work 6 rows raised treble rib as for neck edging, or knit in single rib.

WELT

Join side and sleeve seams as one. With 4.50mm crochet hook, join M to a side seam, pick up the vertical strands and work 1 row tr round front and back, join with a ss, 2ch, turn.
Work 3 rows raised treble rib, joining with a ss and turning on each row. Fasten off. (Or knit in single rib as for neck.)

Creating texture

Interesting textures can quite easily be introduced into Tunisian crochet and numerous variations and combinations are available to the crochet worker who likes to experiment.

The one important point to understand is that Tunisian crochet is initially a complete row of unfinished ordinary crochet stitches. Once the loops have been picked up, the stitches can then be finished off as though they formed an extended, or enlarged, long treble.

With this knowledge, anyone with a working understanding of crochet can produce the same sort of textural combinations as they do with ordinary crochet and the landscape picture, shown on page 20, uses all these techniques. I chose mohair as the main yarn because it reflects and refracts the light, and this enhances the colour blending. The landscape collage has no stitch-by-stitch pattern, but is just my personal use of colours and stitches to achieve an effect.

TUNISIAN BOUCLÉ STITCH

At regular intervals across the pick-up row, work one unfinished double treble by taking the yarn round the hook twice before inserting it into the next vertical thread, yoh and pull a loop through to the front, *yoh, pull through 2 loops on hook, rep from * once

more thus leaving one loop on the hook. On the take-off row, when the loops are taken off in the normal manner (as in simple stitch) the extra long loops created by wrapping the yarn over before inserting into the work will bend towards the front and form small bumps, (see Fig 9).

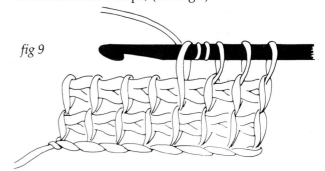

fig 9

TUNISIAN BOX STITCH

In the above pattern the tunisian double treble is worked into the vertical loop in the same row as all the other stitches. In the Tunisian box stitch, the Tunisian long treble (ie. wrapping yarn 1 or more times round hook before inserting into work) is worked into the lowest vertical strand below the one normally used. This leaves the long treble lying flat on top of the work, (see Fig 10). Exactly where the hook is inserted, depends upon the length of the treble being made. As a general rule Tunisian double treble will be inserted and anchored two rows below, a Tunisian triple treble will be anchored three rows below, and a Tunisian quadruple treble will be anchored four rows below.

fig 10

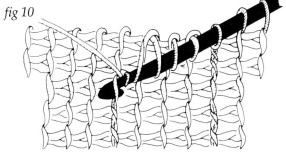

TUNISIAN DROP STITCH

This gives a similar effect as box stitch, but instead of a thick cord like stitch dividing the stripes into rectangles, a flatter two strand 'V' shape makes the division, (see Fig 11).

To work a drop stitch continue in simple stitch to the point where a long dividing point is needed. Insert hook through the fabric from front to back, as though working ordinary crochet (that is not picking up the vertical strand as in simple stitch). Pull the yarn through from the back to the front of the work. Lift the strand until it lies quite flat against the crochet. It should be sufficiently loose not to pucker the work and at the same time not so loose that it does not give a straight line. Just a point to remember–do not work into the vertical strand lying immediately behind the

fig 11

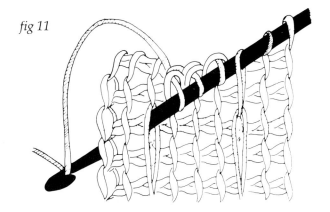

dropped stitch, or an increase will be made. In fact, I always count my stitches at this point. On the next pick up row insert the hook between *both* vertical loops of the drop stitch instead of under them.

TUNISIAN CROSS STITCH

I have found that the cross stitch is best worked between rows of Tunisian simple stitch. This stitch has a tendency to pull the work in and make it quite narrow. One further point – it is necessary to work the cross stitch on the row *after* the one on which you intend to have the crossed stitches, (see Fig 12).

To work the actual cross stitch, *miss one stitch, insert hook under next vertical strand, yoh, pull through to the front leaving the loop on hook, insert hook under vertical strand just missed, yoh, pull through to the front, rep from * to last st, pick up last st. This process causes the strands of the row below to cross, *not* the ones on the Tunisian hook.

fig 12

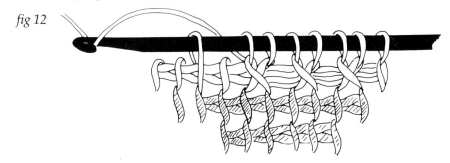

Landscape
The use of the 'tweed' effect in Tunisian crochet is ideal for colour blending

Slipper socks
Bright colours in a smooth yarn make colourful slipper socks, which are attached
to sheepskin soles

Cushions in textured patterns

The four textured patterns given in this section are the ideal choice for hard- wearing and colourful cushion covers.

The green and white cushion, (see page 12), uses a chenille yarn and simple stitch for two rows, combined with a smooth Aran yarn for the cross stitch pattern. The matching pair of cushions using drop stitch and box stitch patterns were worked in chenille in two strongly contrasting colours, (see page 12).

Edge-to-edge Jacket

A variation of Tunisian box stitch is used to create the colourful textured stripes on the yoke and sleeves of this attractive jacket, (see page 24).

Materials: 450g of DK flecked slub yarn (M); 100g of DK in contrast (A); 50 g of contrast (B); 50g of contrast (C); (or any equivalent qualities which will give the same tension); one 6.00mm Tunisian hook; one 4.50mm crochet hook.

Size: to fit 36″ (92cm) bust loosely. To increase or reduce the size, add or subtract 12 sts on the foundation row. When dividing at the underarms, allow 6 sts more, or less, for the back and 3 sts for each front.

Tension: 7 sts = 2″ (5cm) on 6.00mm Tunisian hook.

BODY

With 6.00mm hook and M make 152 ch. Work 40 rows Ts, or required length to underarm, and divide for armholes.

RIGHT FRONT

Work 13 rows Ts on the first 38 sts for the right front, then commence yoke patt.

Row 1: Ts in M.

Row 2: In B, 1Ts, *1Ttr into st below next Ts, 2Ts, rep from * to end.

Row 3: Ts in M.

Row 4: In C, *1Ttr in B row, 2Ts, rep from * to last st, 1Ts in last st.

Row 5: Ts in M.

Row 6: In A, *2Ts, 1Ttr in C row, rep from * to last st, 1Ts in last st.

Row 7: Ts in M.

Row 8: In C, as row 2.

Row 9: Ts in M.

Row 10: In B, as row 4. **

Row 11: Work 1dc over next 6 sts for neck, Ts in M. (32 sts).

Row 12: In C, as row 4.

Row 13: Ts in M.

Row 14: As row 6.

Row 15: Ts in M.

Row 16: In C, as row 2.

Row 17: Ts in M. Break off yarn.

BACK

Rejoin M to next st from front and work 13 rows Ts on the next 76 sts for back. Commence yoke patt.

Row 1: Ts in M, and on all subsequent odd numbered rows.

Row 2: In B, as row 6 of right front.

Row 4: In C, as row 2 of right front.

Row 6: In A, as row 4 of right front.

Row 8: In C, as row 6 of right front.

Row 10: In B, as row 2 of right front.

Row 12: In C, as row 4 of right front.

Row 14: In A, as row 6 of right front.

Row 16: In C, as row 2 of right front.

Row 17: Ts in M. Break off yarn.

LEFT FRONT

Rejoin M to next st from back. Work as given for right front to **.

Row 11: Ts in M, leaving last 6 sts unworked for neck.
Continue in patt on rem 32 sts to correspond with right front.

SLEEVES (MAKE 2)

With 6.00mm Tunisian hook and M make 57 ch.
Work 26 rows in Ts.
Work in patt as given for back for 17 rows. Fasten off.
Turn sleeve upside down. With RS facing, M and 6.00mm Tunisian hook, pick up 57 loops using the vertical strands formed in the foundation row. Continue in patt as given for back, working rows 2 to 17 inclusive. Fasten off.

TO MAKE UP

Join sleeves to armholes of jacket, leaving shoulder seams open and making sure the stripes match exactly.
With Rs facing, B and 4.50mm crochet hook, ss the two pieces together, joining the sleeve and shoulder seam as one, leaving 12dc in centre for back neck. Work 1 row crab st, with Rs facing.
With Rs facing, M and 4.50mm crochet hook work 1 row dc along base of jacket, using st for st.
With Rs of sleeve facing, M and 4.50mm crochet hook, work 34 dc along cuff edge, working one dc for every 2 row ends. Work 3 rows dc, then 1 row crab st, with Rs facing.
With Rs of jacket facing, M and 4.50mm crochet hook work in dc up right front edge, working approximately one st per row end, 2dc at corner, dc round neck, 2dc at corner, dc down left front edge. With Rs facing work 1 row crab st. Fasten off.

Slipper-socks

These warm and hard-wearing slipper-socks are boldly striped and textured. You can use as many oddments of the same thickness of yarn as you have available, (see page 21).

Materials: Oddments of DK yarn in 8 contrasting colours; one 6.00mm Tunisian hook; one 4.00mm crochet hook; 2 soles cut from sheepskin oddments – to make these draw round own feet, punch holes about 3/8″ (1cm) apart, noting that both soles should have the same number of holes.

Size: To fit size of sole made. To lengthen the top of the leg, work more rows Ts after point marked with **.

Tension: 6 sts = 2″ (5cm) on 6.00mm Tunisian hook.

SLIPPER-SOCK (MAKE 2)

With 6.00mm hook and first colour make 37 ch.
Work 2 rows Ts.

Next row: In 2nd colour, *1Tdtr, 1Ts, rep from * to end.
Work 2 rows Ts in first colour.

Next row: In 3rd colour, *1Ts, 1Ttr, rep from * to last 2 sts, 1Ts.
Work 1 row Ts in first colour.
Work 2 rows Ts in 4th colour.

Next row: In 5th colour, *1Ttr, 1Ts, rep from * to end. **
Work 1 row Ts in 5th colour, dec one st each end.
Work 2 rows Ts in 6th colour, dec one st each end of both rows. 31 sts.

INSTEP

Work 2 rows Ts in 6th colour over central 11 sts.

Summer jacket
The use of texture as well as colour has been incorporated in the yoke and sleeve detail

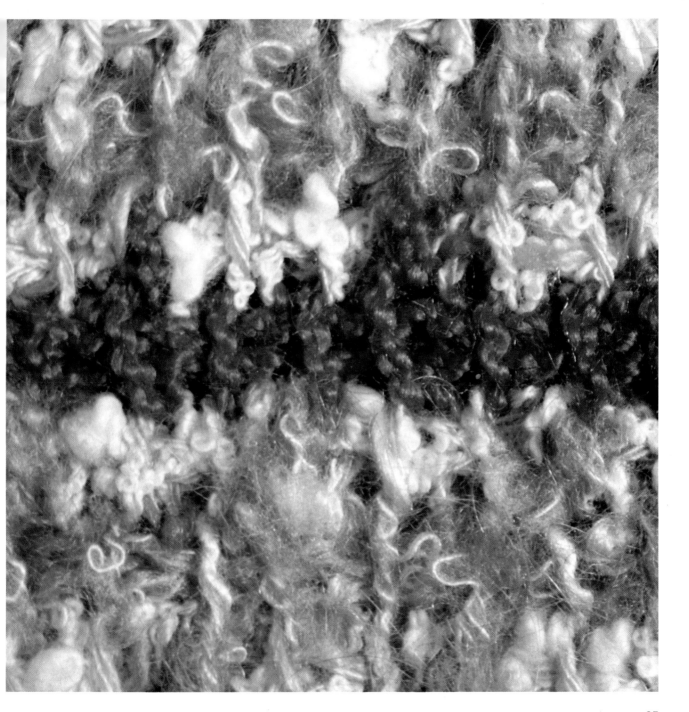

Next row: In 7th colour, *1Tdtr, 1Ts, rep from * to end.
Work 2 rows Ts in first colour.

Next row: In 3rd colour, *1Ts, 1Ttr, rep from * to last 2 sts, 1Ts.
Work 2 rows Ts in 8th colour.

Next row: In 7th colour, *1Tdtr, 1Ts, rep from * to end.
Work 3 rows Ts in first colour. This completes instep.

SIDE FOOT BORDER

In 6th colour work 3 rows Ts from centre back, round foot to centre back. Unless a flexi-hook is being used, it will be necessary to work the border in two halves, linking the 2nd half to the first at the toe. Fasten off. Join seam at back.

FOOT

With 4.00mm crochet hook and 6th colour, work 2 to 4dc into each hole punched in sole, join with ss. Attach to Tunisian fabric by working dc through sts in sole and stitches in sock. Fasten off.

SOCK TOP

With 4.00mm crochet hook and 6th colour, work 1 row tr round top edge, using vertical strands. (For a snug fit, work this over round elastic).
Work 3 rows raised tr rib, see welt of Cross-over top page 14. Fasten off.

Mohair Waistcoat

This design can be made in one colour but it will not be as effective as our example, which blends 8 different colours, (see page 17). When colour blending, oddments of yarn can be used but for this design make sure that you have a total quantity of about 300g, allowing approximately 75g of M and 50g of A.

Materials: About 300g of 78% long hair mohair in Ddk thickness; one 10.00mm Tunisian hook; one 7.00mm and one 6.00mm crochet hook; 5 buttons.

Size: To fit 32-38″ (81-97cm) bust.

Tension: 4 Ts = 2″ (5cm) noting that it is essential to achieve this tension working with a 10.00mm hook.

BODY

With 10.00mm hook and M make 30 ch beg at centre back and work to underarm side edge. Work 1 row Ts.

Next row: Pick up with M. Join in A. Take off with A. Work 1 row Ts with A.

Next row: Pick up with A. Join in B (dark contrast). Take off with B.

Next row: Pick up with B. **Join in C (soft colour). Take off with C, make 40 ch to go over shoulder and form front.

Next row: With C, pick up 40 sts along the ch including loop already on hook, pick up next st in normal way, *1Tdtr placed in st 2 rows below, 2Ts, rep from * to last 2 sts, 1Tdtr in st 2 rows below, 1Ts. Join in M. Take off in M.

Next row: With M, work across 40 sts picked up from ch, *1Ttdr in st 2 rows below, 2Ts, rep from * to end. Join in D. Take off in D.
Work 1 row Ts.

Next row: Pick up with D. Join in E (bright colour). Take off with E.

Next row: Pick up with E. Join in F. Take off with F.

Next row: With F, pick up *1Ts, 1Ttr worked in row below, rep from * to end. Join in G, keep F still attached. Take off in G.

Next row: Pick up with G. Take off with F.

Next row: With G, pick up *1Ts, 1Ttr in row below, rep from * to end. Take off with F. Join in A. Work 1 row Ts with A.

Next row: Pick up with A. Join in E. Take off with E. Join in C.

Work 1 row Ts with C. Break off all yarns. This completes half of the pattern of the waistcoat front and back.

Rejoin M to the foundation ch of the first side and work 2nd side as for first side to **.

With C, make 40 ch before taking off the loops already on the hook, noting that this gives a front extension to correspond with first side. Take off with C.

Next row: Count loop on hook as first Ts, *1Tdtr placed in st 2 rows below, 2Ts, rep from * to st before ch, 1Ts in last st worked, pick up 40 loops along ch, join in M, take off all loops on hook.

Next row: *2Ts (loop on hook counts as one at beg), 1Tdtr in st 2 rows below, rep from * to end of main part of work, cont picking up to end.

Complete as given for first side.

Change to 7.00mm crochet hook. With Rs facing and M, work 1 row dc to end picking up vertical strands. Work in crab st through first 18 sts of back and front together to join side seams, cont working crab st round armhole. 34 sts. Work other side in same way.

FRONTS

With Rs of work facing, shape front edge and beg at base of right front. With 10.00mm Tunisian hook and C, pick up 28 loops, join in B, take off in B. Pick up 24 loops in B, join in C, take off in C.

Next row: Pick up with C, *2Ts, 1Ttr worked in st in row below, rep from * until 21 loops are on hook, join in M, take off in M.

Next row: With M, count loop on hook as 1Ts, *1Ttr in row below, 2Ts, rep from * until 18 loops are on hook, join in A, take off with A.

Next row: Pick up 16 loops with A, take off with A. Break off yarn.

Work second side as first side, reversing all shapings by picking up and taking off in the normal way, then slip st, using vertical loops, over number of sts no longer in use. On the first shaping, slip st over 4 to reduce loops from 28 to 24.

FRONT BORDER

With 7.00mm crochet hook and Rs facing, join in M at base of right front, work in dc into each st, using vertical loops, up front edge, work 9 sts across back neck, work in dc down left front. Work 1 row dc, dec 3 sts across neck line, checking that both sides of waistcoat have same number of sts in border.

With 6.00mm crochet hook and M make 2ch, work in tr to end, noting that there should be sufficient tr at this point to avoid holes where the welt is being connected to the main body of the waistcoat.

Join in C to beg of row just worked, 2 ch, work in raised tr rib, 65 sts in all, see welt of Cross-over top, page 16. (If you have too many tr on first row, dec by inserting hook round 2tr when making a raised tr at the front. Calculate dec so that they are even – I needed to dec every 4th st.) *Turn work.*

With M work 1 row raised tr rib.

Return to C and work another row of raised tr rib.

Continue turning work on every 2 rows, alternating colours M and C, until required length of rib is reached, finishing with Rs facing and M.

Complete by working crab st up the edge of the welt on left side of waistcoat, then up left front, across neck, down right front until the shaping point has been reached, work 5 evenly spaced button loops by working 2 ch between 2 crab sts and missing a st. Fasten off all ends. Sew on 5 buttons to match 5 button loops.

Snug hat or Ski cap

This design uses Tunisian simple stitch and a double ended Tunisian hook is needed to work the contrasting borders round the face and neck, see page 29. You can wear it as a snug-fitting hat, (see Fig 13a), or as a wind-proof ski cap, (see Fig 13b).

Pram rugs
Embroidered cross stitch creates an attractive design worked on to a base of
Tunisian simple stitch

Ski cap
A Tunisian hook is used to make a circle for the crown, and a double-ended
hook is used to create the slight texture in the colour contrast

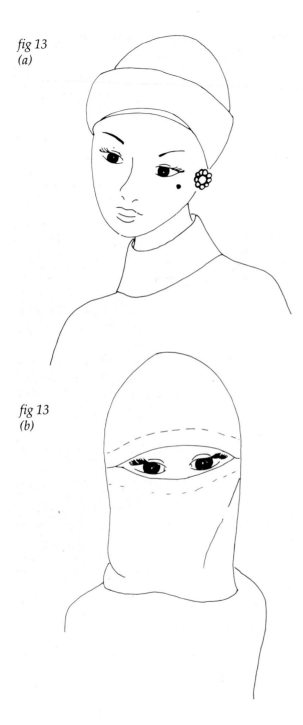

fig 13 (a)

fig 13 (b)

Materials: 100g of lightweight acrylic DK plus a small amount of contrast colour; one 8.00mm double ended Tunisian hook; one 6.00mm crochet hook.

Size: To fit an average adult head.

Tension: 6 sts = 2″ (5cm) worked on 8.00mm Tunisian hook.

CROWN

With 8.00mm Tunisian hook and main yarn make 10 ch.

Row 1: Pick up 2 loops, take off 2 loops.

Row 2: Pick up 3 loops, take off 3 loops.

Row 3: Pick up 4 loops, take off 4 loops.
Continue in this way until all 10 ch have been used. Work another 5 wedges on to this in the same way, (see Fig 14), then carefully graft together to form a circle. Break off yarn.

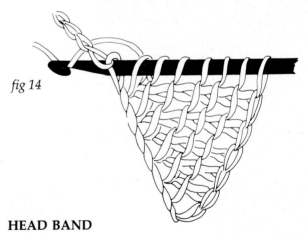

fig 14

HEAD BAND

With 8.00mm Tunisian hook and main yarn make 9 ch.

Next row: Pick up 7 loops (8 loops on hook), insert hook into last ch *and* ch edge of first row at seam of crown, yoh, pull through crown st and ch. Take off loops as normal.
Work in Ts connecting each row to each crown row. Join by grafting.

**With Rs facing and main colour, pick up one loop for each row end (56 loops).
Take off loops in contrast colour, using other end of Tunisian hook. (It will be necessary to remove some loops before completing the row.) Turn work. Pick up in contrast colour. Take off in main colour.**
Repeat from ** to ** once more.

Next row: With main, pick up 18 loops, 20dc, 18 loops. With contrast colour take off 18 loops, make 20ch, 18 loops.

Next row: Pick up in contrast colour, take off in main.

Next row: Pick up in main, take off in contrast.

Next row: Pick up in contrast, take off in main. Join seam carefully.

CHIN BAND

With 8.00mm Tunisian hook and main yarn make 12 ch.

Next row: Pick up 10 loops (11 loops on hook), insert hook into last ch *and* vertical st at side of join, yoh, pull through st and ch. Take off loops as normal. Work from ** to ** once as given for head band. Change to 6.00mm crochet hook. Work 1 row dc using vertical strands. Join seam. Fasten in all ends. With contrast colour, work 1 row dc round eye opening to neaten edge.

Cross stitch embroidery

Tunisian simple stitch forms a fabric with clearly defined squares showing on the right side. Once the fabric has been worked, it is easy to apply cross stitch embroidery to give a decorative effect. It is essential not to pull the yarn too tightly when working the embroidery, as this will distort the fabric. For position of needle insertions when working cross stitch, (see Fig 15a and b).
The pram rug is worked in a soft cotton yarn and embroidered in a contrasting colour, (see page 28). The contrast colour is used to work an edging all round the rug.

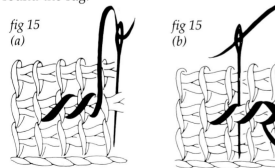

fig 15
(a)

fig 15
(b)

Materials: 100g of soft cotton DK plus one ball of contrast for embroidery and edging; one 7.00mm Tunisian hook; one 5.50mm crochet hook; tapestry needle.

Size: 18″ × 22″ (45 × 55cm).

Tension: 6 sts = 2″ (5cm).

Pram rug

With 7.00mm Tunisian hook and main yarn make 45 ch. Work approximately 55 rows Ts, or until work measures 20″ (51cm) from beg.
With 5.50mm crochet hook and contrast colour, work one round dc round all edges, working 2dc into each corner, join with a ss, 1 ch turn.

Round 2: Work in dc to end, working 3dc into corner sts, join with a ss, turn.

Round 3: Rs is now facing, work in crab st to end. Fasten off.
Embroider motif in one corner. Back with iron-on cotton.

ABBREVIATIONS

beg	begin(ning)
ch	chain(s)
cm	centimetre(s)
dc	double crochet (US single crochet)
dec	decrease
DK	double knitting
DdK	double double knitting
dtr	double treble (US treble)
fig	figure
g	gram
htr	half treble
"	inch(es)
inc	increase
lp(s)	loop(s)
M	main colour
mm	millimetre(s)
patt	pattern
pur	pick up row
quad tr	quadruple treble (US triple treble)
rem	remain(ing)
rep	repeat
Rs	right side of work
ss	slip stitch
st(s)	stitch(es)
tog	together
tor	take off row
tr	treble (US double crochet)
Tdtr	Tunisian double treble (US treble)
Ts	Tunisian simple stitch
Ttr	Tunisian treble (US double crochet)
yoh	yarn over hook

SUPPLIERS

Your local wool shop should be able to help you with suitable yarns for the designs in this book. Should you experience any difficulty in obtaining your requirements, however, these can be ordered by post from the following address:
Crochet Design Centre,
White Cross, South Road, Lancaster, LA1 4HX.

Acknowledgements

Tunisian Crochet

First published in Great Britain 1987
Search Press Ltd.,
Wellwood, North Farm Road,
Tunbridge Wells, Kent TN2 3DR

Copyright © 1987 Search Press Ltd.

Text by Pauline Turner
Designs by Pauline Turner, Helen Barnes, Mary Cheadle.

Photographs by Search Press Studios.

ISBN 0 85532 598 4

Typeset by Scribe Design, 123 Watling Street, Gillingham, Kent.
Made and printed in Spain by A.G. Elkar, S. Coop., Bilbao 12